ENTRY IN AN UNKNOWN HAND

Books by Franz Wright

Poetry
Tapping the White Cane of Solitude
The Earth Without You
8 Poems
*The One Whose Eyes Open When You Close
        Your Eyes*
Going North in Winter
Entry in an Unknown Hand

Translations
Wandering by Hermann Hesse (with James
        Wright)
Jarmilla. Flies: 10 Prose Poems by Erica Pedretti
The Life of Mary by Rainer Maria Rilke
The Unknown Rilke
No Siege is Absolute by René Char

ENTRY IN AN UNKNOWN HAND

poems by

Franz Wright

Carnegie Mellon University Press

Pittsburgh 1989

Acknowledgments

Acknowledgment is gratefully made to the editors of the following journals, where most of these poems first appeared: *Blades, Columbia Magazine, Crazyhorse, Field, Ironwood, The Paris Review, Ploughshares, Quarry West, Raccoon, Shankpainter, Tri Quarterly, The Virginia Quarterly Review.*

"Winter Entries" was originally published on broadsides by Brita Bergland.

A number of these poems also appeared in chapbooks titled *Going North in Winter* (Gray House Press) and *Entry in an Unknown Hand* (published by Martha McCollough, Minatoby Press).

Anthologies in which some of these poems have appeared or will appear:
The Ploughshares Poetry Reader
Amnesis
The Longman Anthology of Contemporary American Poetry

I would like to thank the Provincetown Fine Arts Work Center and the National Endowment for the Arts for writing fellowships which helped make possible the completion of this book.

--F.W.

The publication of this book is supported by a grant from the Pennsylvania Council on the Arts.

Contents

I

UNTITLED

Will I always be eleven,
lonely in this house,
reading books
that are too hard for me,
in the long fatherless hours.
The terrible hours of the window,
the rain-light
on the page,
awaiting the letter,
the phone call,
still your strange elderly child.

WINTER: TWILIGHT & DAWN

Buson said the winter rain
shows what is before our eyes
as though it were long ago.
I have been thinking about it for days,
and now I see.
And as I write the hills are turning green.
It does that here. The hills turn slowly
green in the interminable rain of late November,
as though time had begun
running backward
into a cold and unheard of summer.
How alone we are here,
you have no idea.
We are as far from you as stars, as those white
herons standing on the shore,
growing more distinct
as night comes on . . .

What a black road this is.
Orion nailed there
upside down, and banking right
into the cloud and descending
behind Mount Konocti;
the lake our bodies
slowly strummed awake
healed over, still.
And there is someone who is farther, and even more alone.
Once I resolved to remind myself—each hour I live
is one hour of his death,
but I have forgotten. I have forgotten,
hour of departure, when *all* are sleeping;
hour I love, first light, first
wind.
Oaks in the starless wind.

Clearlake, California

ROOMS

Rooms I (I will not say
worked in) once heard in. Words
my mouth heard,
then—be
with me. Rooms,
you open onto one
another in the mind: still house
this life, be in me
when I leave, don't take from me
what took so long.

THE CRAWDAD

for Dzvinia

The crawdad absorbed in minute excavations;
trees leaning over the water, the breathing
everywhere. And watching alone,
a door I have walked through
into a kinder
and more intelligent world—,
my face looking back at me, under the water
moss glowing faintly on stone.
We will not sleep, we will be changed.

JOSEPH COME BACK AS THE DUSK
(1950-1982)

The house is cold. It's raining,
getting dark. That's Joseph

for you: it's that time
of the day again.

We had been drinking, oddly enough.
He left.

I thought, a walk—
It's lovely to walk.

His book and glasses on the kitchen table.

THE WORDS

All day I slept
and woke and slept

again, the square
of winter sky lighting

the room,
which had grown

octaves
grayer . . .

What to do, if the words disappear as you write—
what to do

if they remain,
and you disappear.

TO THE HAWK

In the unshaded hill
where you kill
every day I have climbed
for a glimpse of you; below me
all the earth turned
golden
in the searing wind,
its abrupt blast
at a bend in the road
as I approach the summit, shining
wind, where you live,
cloaked in your cruel and victorious
nimbus of fire, floating, suspended
someplace out past
visibility:
        eyes
kissed by a speech beyond words—
beholding themselves in the sun.

AUDIENCE

The street deserted. Nobody,
only you and one last
dirt colored robin,
fastened to its branch
against the wind. It seems
you have arrived
late, the city unfamiliar,
the address lost.
And you made such a serious effort—
pondered the obstacles deeply,
tried to be your own critic.
Yet no one came to listen.
Maybe they came, and then left.
After you traveled so far,
just to be there.
It was a failure, that is what they will say.

ALCOHOL

You do look a little ill.

But we can do something about that, now.

Can't we.

The fact is you're a shocking wreck.

Do you hear me.

You aren't all alone.

And you could use some help today, packing in the
dark, boarding buses north, putting the seat back and
grinning with terror flowing over your legs through
your fingers and hair . . .

I was always waiting, always here.

Know anyone else who can say that.

My advice to you is think of her for what she is:
one more name cut in the scar of your tongue.

What was it you said, "To rather be harmed than
harm, is not abject."

Please.

Can we be leaving now.

We like bus trips, remember. Together

we could watch these winter fields slip past, and
never care again,

think of it.

I don't have to be anywhere.

AT THE END OF
THE UNTRAVELED ROAD

Under Konocti
the long eucalyptus lined
road in the moon,
wind of November,
the now hawkless
hills
     turning green—
it was always here, not yet remembered.

Whatever it is

I was seeking, with my useless despair:
it was always here.
And I'm on my way now,
the pages too heavy to turn,
the first morning lights coming on
over the lake. How happy I am!
There's no hope for me.

II

VERMONT CEMETERY

Drowsy with the rain
and late October sun, remember,
we stopped to read the names.
A mile across the valley

a little cloud of sheep
disappeared over a hill,
a little crowd of sleep—. . .
time to take a pill

and wake up,
and drive through the night.
Once I spoke your name,
but you slept on and on.

MORNING ARRIVES

Morning arrives
unannounced
by limousine: the tall
emaciated chairman

of sleeplessness in person
steps out on the sidewalk
and donning black glasses, ascends
the stairs to your building

guided by a German shepherd.
After a couple faint knocks
at the door, he slowly opens
the book of blank pages

pointing out
with a pale manicured finger
particular clauses,
proof of your guilt.

NORTH COUNTRY ENTRIES

Do you still know these early leaves, trans-
lucent, shining, spreading on their branches
like green flames?

And the hair-raising stars flowing over the
ridge late at night . . .

No one home in the house by itself on the
pine-hidden road,

or the 4-story barn up the road, leaning on
its hill.

The two horses who've opened the gate to their
field, old, wandering around on the lawn.

The sky becoming ominous.

Which is more awful, a sentient or endlessly
presenceless sky?

BIRTHDAY

I make my way down the back stairs
in the dark. I know
it sounds crude to admit it,
but I like to piss in the back yard.

You can be alone for a minute
and look up at the stars,
and when you return
everyone is there.

You get drunker, and listen to records.
Everyone agrees.
The dead singers have the best voices.
At four o'clock in the morning

the dead singers have the best voices.
And I can hear them now,
as I climb the stairs
in the dark I know.

THE NOTE

for C. D.

Summer is summer remembered;

a light on upstairs at the condemned orphanage,

an afternoon storm coming.

She heard a gun go off and one hair turned gray.

Somehow I will still know you.

THE TALK

Aged a lot during our talk
(you were gone).
Left and wandered the streets for some hours—
melodramatic, I know—
poor, crucified by my teeth.

And yet, how we talked
for a while.
All those things we had wanted to say for so long,
yes—I sat happily nodding
my head in agreement,
but you were gone.
In the end it gets discouraging.

I had let myself in;
I'd sat down in your chair.
I could just see you reading late
in the soft lamp light—
looking at a page,

listening to its voice:

yellow light shed in circles, in stillness,
all about your hair . . .

ILL LIT

Leaves stir overhead;
I write what I'm given to write.

The extension cord to the black house.

WORD FROM HOME

Then I went out among the dead
a pint of whiskey in my head
and lay on a mound
covered with snow,
and closing my eyes to the blowing snow

looked into his face.

Smiling and wincing,
reading his shoes,
holding out a ruined hand;
wishing for a way to disappear—
all the poor formalities of the mad.

As if I had met him, years later,
an accident—something is wrong with his face.
Thinner, perhaps, the eyes cruel
with pain, my own
reflection in a knife . . .

The look of love gives the face beauty.

We look at him
as if he were a stain.

We look at him

ENTRY IN AN UNKNOWN HAND

And still nothing happens. I am not arrested.
By some inexplicable oversight

nobody jeers when I walk down the street.

I have been allowed to go on living in this
room. I am not asked to explain my presence
anywhere.

What posthypnotic suggestions were made; and
are any left unexecuted?

Why am I so distressed at the thought of taking
certain jobs?

They are absolutely shameless at the bank—
you'd think my name meant nothing to them. Non-
chalantly they hand me the sum I've requested,

but I know them. It's like this everywhere—

they think they are going to surprise me: I,
who do nothing but wait.

Once I answered the phone, and the caller hung up—
very clever.

They think that they can scare me.

I am always scared.

And how much courage it requires to get up in the
morning and dress yourself. Nobody congratulates
you!

At no point in the day may I fall to my knees and
refuse to go on, it's not done.

I go on

dodging cars that jump the curb to crush my hip,

accompanied by abrupt bursts of black-and-white
laughter and applause,

past a million unlighted windows, peered out at
by the retired and their aged attack-dogs—

toward my place,

the one at the end of the counter,

the scalpel on the napkin.

DURATION

On the sill
the blown-out candle

burning
in the past . . .

Frozen clouds
passing over

the border
north. Listen

to the end,
listen with me.

Woodstock, Vermont

III

NO LONGER OR NOT YET

(from a phrase by Hermann Broch)

In the gray temples of business

In the famine of the ant-bewitched seed

Wolves attacking people in the half-deserted suburbs

And kings dead with their hands crossed on their genitals
        a thousand years from now

In sunlight shining on an open Bible

In the answering machine home computer and flesh-colored
        limousine

In the sneer and the kick in the face world without end

In my crouched shadow loping beside me

In the imbecilic prose of my thoughts

In the voice of the one fingerprinted blindfolded and
        shot

World of dead parents unconsciously aped without end

In the hand above the rainbow horses of the Pech-Merle
        cave walls

We interrupt this program to bring you the announcement
        that enemy ICBMs will begin to arrive in
        10 minutes

In the eeriness which corridors and stairwells have for
        children

Death of the weekday

In their parties alone in a sip from an empty cup

In the little grass toad beating in your palm

The spider spinning in the dust the barren worm

The death of tears

In the gashed vivid colors of gas station restrooms
        at three in the morning

(And we thank Thee for destroying the destroyers of the
        world)

In the unaccompanied boy on the Greyhound the old woman
        with a balloon

World no longer or not yet

The moon which goes dragging the ocean and turning
        its chalky steppes away

Unsummonable world

In the white stars in the black sky shining in the
        past

The black words in the white page uttered long ago

Death of tears

In the storm of wordless voices the hand abruptly
        shocked into dictation

(Envelop me clothe me in blackness book closed)

In early March crocuses pushing deafly through soil

While you quietly turn between dreams like a page

The morning light standing in the room like someone
        who has returned after long absence
        younger

World no longer or not yet

IV

LOOK INTO ITS EYES

The leaved wind,

the leaved wind
in the mirror

and windows, perceived
by the one-week-old . . .

Forever, we weren't here—

BIOGRAPHY

The light was getting bad;
he wished the rain would stop.

He'd try again tomorrow—
anyway, he had to walk.

Brain-sick. Wet pavement. Green neon.

The light was getting awful—
had to walk the ghost . . .

He'd try again, he wished.
He'd try again.

THE DAY

My mother picks me up at school.
Strange. I leave the others playing,
walk to where she's parked—
and why are we driving so slowly?

You have to turn right here, she whispers.
When we get there the whole house is silent.
Why's that? Does this mean
I can watch The Three Stooges?

Evidently. She's driving away now
and he is not typing downstairs:
he isn't there at all, I've checked.
This must be my lucky day.

WRITING AT NIGHT

The sound of someone crying in the next apartment.

In an unfamiliar city, where I find myself once
more

unprepared for this specific situation

or any situation whatsoever, now—

frozen in the chair,

my body one big ear.

A big ear crawling up a wall.

In the room where I quietly rave and gesticulate—
and no one must hear me—
alone until sleep:

my life a bombed site turning green again . . .

The sound of someone crying

THERE

(T. F.)

Let it start to rain,
the streets are empty now.
Over the roof hear the leaves
coldly conversing in whispers;
a page turns in the book
left open by the window.
The streets are empty, now
it can begin. I am not there.

Like you
I wasn't present
at the burial. This morning

I have walked out
for the first time
and wander here
among the blind
flock of names
standing still
in the rain—

(the one on your stone
will remain
listed in telephone books
for a long time, I guess, light
from a disappeared star . . .)

— just to locate the place,
to come closer, without knowing where you are
or if you know I am there.

Oberlin

POEM
for Frank Bidart

Per each dweller
one grass blade, one leaf
one apartment
one shadow
one rat.

By itself, defending a lost position,

the poem
            writing the poet . . .

Anvil of solitude

So diminish the city's population
by one, and go
add your tear to the sea—

Heart that wonderfully lasted
                        until
I learned how to write
what it so longed to say

Nothing of the kind.

A DAY COMES

A day comes
when it has always been winter,
will always be winter.
Witnesses said the crowd fled
through the park, chased by policemen on horseback
past the Tomb of the Unknown
Soldier as the guard
was being changed,
but they are gone.
The witnesses are gone.
A day comes
when the planet stops turning.
It is February here,
late afternoon.
It will always be late afternoon,
neither dark nor light out.
But we cannot be bothered,
because we are asleep;
the door is locked.
Now and then somebody comes and knocks
and goes away again
back down the hall,
back down the stairs.
But we cannot be bothered,
because we are asleep
and listening, listening.
Listen.
Do you hear the wind?
We have always been asleep,
will always be asleep—
turning over
like pages on fire . . .

Where were we?
We were listening.
No, I don't hear it either.
The wind, the marching
boots, the burning
names.

New York

RILKE: THREE DISCARDED FRAGMENTS

Who can say, when I go to a window,
that someone near death doesn't
turn his eyes in my direction
and stare and groan and, dying, feed on me.
That in this very house the forsaken
face isn't lifted, that needs me now

•

That smile, for a long time
I couldn't describe it—
the velvet depression
left by a jewel . . .

•

A child's soul like a leaf light still shines through

THE STREET

On it lives one bird

who commences singing, for some reason best
known to itself, at precisely 4 a.m.

Each day I listen for it in the night.

I too have a song to say alone,

but can't begin. On it, surrounded by blocks of
black warehouses,

is located this room. I say this room, but no
one knows

how many rooms I have. So many rooms how will I
light

so many . . . Also yours, though you are never
there.

It's true I've been gone a long time.

But I have come back. I have.

Where are you?

I can change.

WRITTEN AT 20

I know it isn't true that
after a man is buried his lips go on moving.
That graveclothes can rise to their feet
and come visit,

that they know how to
knock on both doors at once.

I refuse to board the train that carries my
coffin back and forth across America
holding up traffic for four minutes
in the middle of the night in Kent, Ohio.

I have very little time for pilgrimages
through the cathedrals of moonlit barns
where ninety men from the eastern front are dying,
and one young man who isn't Christ, trying to heal them.

And I'd rather not have to write any more of
those foot-in-the-grave letters people
who're suffering write to cripple the fortunate.
The ones that say: I am your friend, believe me,

I'd give you the shroud off my back.

MY WORK

For Jordy Powers

The way I work is strange.

For one thing, you would never call it work.

Although I'm good at that.

Work is not the term . . .

It destroys me, I adore it—

I'll look at it someday and noticing its utility
still fails to surpass that of a lyre locked up in
a glass case tuned an octave above human hearing,

I'll take an ax to it.

I'll stop speaking to it.

I'll sit alone in some shit-hole and inject it
until the jewels roll out of my eyes.

I don't know what all I'll do,

snow of
        unlit afternoon . . .

mute and agreed-to
descent

COORDINATES

Waking up at an improbable hour
in the small gray-lit Boston apartment
where I can never bring myself
to believe I actually live . . .
Going off in the winter morning to teach
certain there's been a mistake,
knowing as I enter the classroom
the students will look in my face
with startled unrecognition,
that before I can utter a word
someone in a suit will appear
and ask me to come with him.

•

This won't hurt at all.
It does?
Well we haven't been taking good care of them,
have we. Difficulty explaining to some
the concept of financial terror—
specifically, that if you're afraid to buy food
if you can help it you are not going to spend
$1500 on a tooth;
difficulty of explaining anything
with your mouth clamped open.
Under anesthesia

I walk along a sunflower field I know of

•

It was still day
when I boarded the train.

The tunnel

then the Charles,
and soft blue lights of traffic in the rain.

•

Everyone in his right mind is asleep.
A black car glides past,
in its wake (the

methedrine blossoming coldly

through fingers and spine)
a prolonged Coltrane scream

and a shiver of beauty open the night

WAITING UP

I can remember you
mentioning once
how you'd wait until your mother was preoccupied
or gone, to dress
the doll all in white
for its little funeral—
how all the while it stared into your eyes
with its cold unbeckonable eyes,
and seemed to smile.
Why this
I couldn't say. And then again
why not? It's easy
to remember anything— . . .
I'll walk now, maybe.
The clouds' stature slumbrously building
and blooming on the horizon,
identityless, huge
gesticulations from the trees,
a bird's voice
hidden back in the leaves,
the remote barely audible wake
from the roar of an airliner's engines
fill the gray morning . . .
Maybe your presence
will startle me now;
maybe I'll rise from
this chair.
Maybe the room will be empty.

The room will be empty,
and you will not come.

GUESTS

Smell of winter apples on the air;
around me night, the wind, Marie, the stars.
Last night I dreamed I stood here,
this very spot—why I've come—
lights on in a house across the valley
where there is no house.
Stood here as I lay beside you
and looked so fondly at those lights
they might have been our home, and why not?
Everyone you see
lives somewhere.
How is this done?

WINTER ENTRIES

Love no one, work, and don't let the pack know
     you're wounded . . .

Stupid, disappointed strategies.

Hazel wind of dusk, I have lived so much.

Friendless eeriness of the new street—

The poem does not come, but its place is kept set.

GOING NORTH IN WINTER

The sound of pines in the wind . . .
And to think you're the only person on earth
isn't hard, at the end
of the long journey nowhere.
Yet in the end I have come to
love this room and be the one
looking out on snowfields, blank
scores of wire fence in the deepening
snow, the wind through them a passage
of remembered music, bare
unbeckoning branches
with never a ghost
of a deciduous rustling,
the stilled river
with the sheet over its face . . .
going north in winter.
And it's all right
to glance out the window:
the fear will grow less
or more intense, but
it will always be there. Unseen
it's a palpable force,
isn't it. Like electricity
which can be employed,
as has been pointed out,
to kill you in a chair
or light your room.
But I'm through with that now.
I reach over and switch on the dark.
It's all right to pronounce a few words
when you're by yourself, and feel a little joy.

Notes

"Rooms" derives from well-known passages in Blanchot, Proust, and Rilke.

The penultimate line of "To the Hawk" is adapted from a sentence in Hart Crane's letters.

The final line of "Audience" is based on a sentence in Kafka's diaries.

Parts of "No Longer Or Not Yet" were suggested by passages in Bruno Bettelheim's *Love Is Not Enough*, Eugene Marais' *The Soul of the White Ant*, Sartre's *Baudelaire*, Barbara Tuchman's *A Distant Mirror*, and *The Book of Revelations*.